Buy to Let

◆

The Key Steps

First published in 2000 by Stewart Ross Publishers Ltd
2nd Edition published in 2002
Reprinted 2004

ISBN 0-9537563-2-7
Buy to Let The Key Steps - copyright 2000 Stewart Ross Publishers Ltd
Key Steps Series - copyright 2000 Stewart Ross Publishers Ltd
keysteps.co.uk - Registered domain name

A catalogue record for this book is available from the British Library

This book has been prepared for general guidance. Laws and regulations
are complex, liable to change and specific to individual countries and
states so readers should check the current position before proceeding with
any arrangements.

Rental returns are never static. Readers are advised to consult a qualified,
experienced Letting Agent to verify the current situation in your area.

CONTENTS

SECTION 1 - KEY STEPS TO BUYING AND LETTING RESIDENTIAL PROPERTY

SECTION 2 - ISSUES THAT REALLY MATTER

SECTION 3 - AVOIDING THE MOST COMMON PITFALLS

ANNEX - FURTHER READING

QUOTES

Kate Short has been investing in properties for almost five years. She said - *"by starting early I have managed to create a portfolio of five properties, re-mortgaging as I have gone along."*

Alan and John Gwynn, both in their early fifties, had £20,000 to invest but felt that putting their money into a Building Society would not give them the return they needed.

"We read about the Buy-to-Let option and contacted an Agent in the Association of Residential Letting Agents. Now, within six weeks, our first tenants have moved in on a 12 month contract. We bought a £70,000 two-bed flat in Bromley and are receiving £500 a month."

Gone are the days when buying residential property to let was considered such a high risk that interest rates on loans were far higher than rates on ordinary mortgages.

In the late 1980's, when the property market was booming, the percentage of rented homes dropped to about 7 per cent.

Today it is more than 11 per cent, which is still tiny compared with France or Germany's 40%.

Key Steps to Buying and Letting Residential Property

The idea of Buy to Let may have attracted your interest because of concerns about your pension or as a way of investing.

Whatever the reason, Section 1 will clearly explain the three key steps you would need to take in order to buy and let residential property, namely :

- ***Deciding on the type of residential rental market to enter***

- ***Identifying the best location to buy a property***

- ***Buying a property and starting letting***

STEP 1

◆

Deciding on the Type of Residential Rental Market to Enter

Two factors will dictate which type of residential rental market you will be able to enter - the **rental levels** and the **amount of day to day involvement that you want**.

How will rental levels affect the type of property you buy ?

Surveys show that there is a wide variation in the average rental returns for different types of properties throughout the UK.

Table 1 -
A comparison of the rental return from different types of property

	Multiplier
House with furnished bedsits	3.0
1 bedroom flat	2.0
2 bedroom flat	1.8
2 bedroom terraced house	1.6
3 bedroom semi	1.3
4 bedroom detached	1.0

Meaning that £200,000 invested in furnished bed-sits would on average yield three times as much rent as the same sum invested in a four bedroom detached house.

These figures are an average throughout the UK, but they do show that choosing the right type of property to rent is very important and, in general, with the exception of bed-sits, the higher the property price the lower the returns on the money invested.

How much day to day involvement do you want ?

Renting property, like any other business, takes time to organise.

Bearing this in mind you need to be realistic about how much time you have available to find the property, prepare it for renting, attract suitable tenants and under-take the management.

It is very easy to underestimate the time needed to:-

- *search out and buy the right property*

- *carry out any renovation and/or decoration work*

- *purchase the furniture and organise delivery .*

To renovate or not to renovate?

The starting point is to decide whether to buy a property which will be ready to let or one that is in need of extensive renovation or redecoration. Your decision will of course be influenced by how much spare time you have and your do-it -yourself skills.

You may well have the contacts to pay someone to do the work for you but remember that redecoration and renovation tends to take a lot more time than you expect.

And time renovating or redecorating means you are losing rental income.

Involvement in finding tenants ?

During the tenant-search period, time will be needed to :-

- *advertise, interview and vet prospective tenants*

- *prepare and agree an inventory with the tenant*

- *liaise with the tenant to agree the contract, the deposit and the rental standing order.*

As you gain experience you will become more competent to manage these steps. But, unless you have someone to call on who can provide sound, professional advice based on many years of experience, it is highly advisable to start by using an agent. *(See Issue 5—Selecting an agent).*

Involvement in managing the tenants ?

Once the property has been successfully let, time will be needed to:-

- *monitor the rental payments and periodically check the condition of the property and furnishings*

- *attend to any problems which might arise*

- *make good any wear and tear or any damage.*

Apart from normal property maintenance or eventualities such as storm damage, the time you will need to manage the tenants will very much depend upon how successful you or your agent is in selecting your tenants.

With good tenants in a block of flats that has a good management company your time and involvement during the tenancy period can be minimal.

But, it is useful to have an arrangement with an agent so that you can ask his advice about any problems that might arise. Again, this will be discussed in *Issue 5- Selecting an agent*.

Another sensible move is to consider joining the management company or committee. This way you will have early warning of any problems that arise connected with your properties.

How will the choice of tenants affect your day to day involvement?

Three groups of tenants stand out as distinct groups :-

1.   Students

Student lets can take a considerable amount of time and effort to manage. The wear and tear tends to be high and considerable damage can occur especially at end of term parties before they leave. But rental returns can be high if you have the time and patience.

The way to cut down the risk is by regular visits so that the tenants are aware that you are checking continuously.

Before launching into student letting you should check whether you come under the regulations for HMOs— "Houses in Multiple Occupation."

These regulations (mentioned in Step 3 - Buying your first property and starting letting) can increase the cost of preparing the property and increase your day to day involvement.

It is also worth checking whether the college or universities in the area have any specific regulations or vetting processes that they go through before including your property on their register.

2. Social Security Tenants

Social Security tenants can provide a reliable source of rental income provided you are aware of the following procedures you have to go through and the potential pitfalls:

- Normally the landlord advertises for and vets the tenants

- Prior to your first let a Social Security Department assessor visits the property to determine the rental level they will fund. The process may take over a month to complete

- Any extra rent over and above this figure will have to be agreed with and paid for by the tenant

- Any deposit will have to be obtained from the tenant which may prove difficult

- Prior to agreeing a contract with the tenant you must make sure that the Social Security payment will be paid to you, not to the tenant

- The tenant submits the paperwork to claim the payments from the Department of Social Security - who will stop the payments if it is not up to date.

   So the tenant must be made aware in the tenancy agreement that he is responsible for the rental payments regardless of whether it is being subsidised by any one else.

3. Young Professional Couples

Young professional couples often both work and usually are good tenants. Statistics show that they prefer to delay having children until they are over 27, so there is less risk of wear and tear. In addition, after 1 to 2 years they will usually wish to buy their own property which is a convenient time to raise the rent if rents are rising

4. Corporate Lets

Blue chip companies seeking to house their employees require high quality properties with furnishings and equipment to match.

Increasingly such companies are prepared to pay for serviced accommodation.

The bonus of such clients is that you are likely to secure tenants who will look after the property but you must be available to respond quickly to the tenants' requests.

True Case Study

Mr. Barker bought his first property to rent mainly because his wife had made very few payments towards her pension. He was concerned that if he died before her his pension would be halved, leaving her insufficient to live on.

He purchased a two bedroom flat with a garage in South Manchester which he now lets to young professional couples.

This choice was made for the following reasons :

- South Manchester is an area with a high demand for renting from professional people

- a high record of car theft in the area necessitated the purchase of a garage with the flat

- an excellent metro service and local facilities would attract tenants, cutting down gaps between tenancies.

Managing the property was simplified by :

- using an agent to advertise, interview and vet new tenants, prepare and agree the inventory, organise the contract, obtain the deposit and set up the payment standing orders

- using the agent as an interface between Mr. Barker and the tenant during the management phase, even though Mr. Barker managed the property himself

- the agent providing advice during the management phase, included in his fee

- letting to young professional couples who do not smoke, have children or pets

- providing good quality furniture and furnishings and charging at the top end of the local rental market in order to attract tenants who are house proud

- getting to know the neighbors adjacent to the property so that they acted as watch dogs.

STEP 2

♦

Identifying the Best Location To Buy a Property.

It is commonly quoted that house prices depend on three things - area, area and area. For rented property the guiding rule is location, location, location.

Good rental income will always be achieved in locations where demand is high, which means the big cities and areas which :

- are pleasant and attractive to live in
- possess good local facilities
- are close to good public transport.

How do rents vary nationally ?

Residential property rentals vary widely depending on where they are in the UK. Average figures in the past are shown in table 2 :-

Table 2 - *A comparison of the rental return in different geographical locations*

	Multiplier
NW of England	1.6
London	1.57
SE England	1.4
Wales	1.1
Scotland	1.0

Meaning that £200,000 invested in a particular type of property in the North West of England would on average yield 1.6 times the rental from £200,000 invested in the same type of property in Scotland

How do you find the most suitable area to buy a property to rent ?

You only have to drive through any big city to notice how rapidly you move from pleasant attractive areas to less desirable areas.

The following points system will help you identify the area to suit the type of tenant that you wish to attract.

The guidelines will only give you a general feel, they do not take into account the wide range of highly undesirable features, such as the existence of council rubbish tips, that you must take into account in your search.

Points can be awarded to a specific area you look at as follows:

Area	Points
Excellent residential area	10
Good residential area	6
Marginal residential area	3

Facilities	Points
Close proximity to:	

Universities or other educational facilities	3
Restaurants	1
Take-aways	1
Launderettes	1
Pubs with atmosphere and/or good decor	1
Pleasant parks	1

Public Transport

Close to a regular bus route	4
Close to a regular metro	5
With reasonable access to an airport or to motorways	3

To pick the right area for the tenants you are seeking, the points quoted below will serve as a good guide to aim at as a minimum :

Student lets	10
Social Security tenants	10
Self-contained bed-sit accommodation	13
Apartments for professionals	15

True Case Study

Suppose you are looking at properties within a city area, close to a university. The area is a bit run down but this is compensated by the number of popular pubs and the frequency of buses.

Points should be allocated as follows :

A marginal residential area	-	allocate 3 points
Close to universities	-	allocate 3 points
Close to good pubs	-	allocate 1 point
Near a bus route	-	allocate 4 points
	TOTAL	11

Looking at properties to purchase in this area it would appear to be suitable for students, social security tenants or mid market bed-sits, but it might not attract professional people prepared to pay higher rents.

STEP 3

♦

Buying Your First Property and Starting Letting.

Choosing a property - points to be aware of ?

Before buying a property there is no substitute for having a building survey carried out by a qualified surveyor, or a survey by a structural engineer.

Even with a survey, knowing the following facts could save you a lot of money :

1. The most important point to remember, is that you are buying and decorating the property to appeal to a tenant, so empty your mind of your own tastes and preferences and speak to as many local letting agents as possible.

2. No matter where you buy, choose a standard property, close to public transport and main roads.

3. Check and re-check that your sums add up. As a rough rule the rent must cover the mortgage payments plus 130 to 150%. The extra needs to cover agent's fees, maintenance/service charges, insurance and periods when the property is unlet, plus some profit.

Beware of old lifts, eroding reinforced concrete, cement render or timber cladding - they can all lead to **BIG** bills.

4. Old buildings cost substantially more to maintain and renovate than new buildings.

5. A well managed block of flats should have a good cash reserve in the management accounts to cover periodic maintenance, such as renewal of flat roofs or lifts.

6. Any heating system over 15 years old is likely to need replacing while under floor or forced-draught heating is not as popular with tenants as gas or electric storage heaters.

7. If at all possible, the property should have a garage or off road parking, especially in an area with a high crime rate.

8. The cost of renovation and redecoration can easily equal the difference in market price between a property ready for occupation and one requiring improvement, especially if you take into account the lost rental while the improvements are carried out.

9. For multiple occupation buildings— check the Local Authority regulations. Fire escape regulations can be very costly.

10. Ground floor flats are more likely to develop problems with damp than flats at a higher level as they get older

What should you be aware of in regard to the location of the rental property ?

1. Remember the importance of the suitability of the area plus availability of local facilities and public transport in selecting where you purchase the property.

2. Open grassed areas attract children, which might not suit all tenants.

3. Many prospective tenants prefer accommodation above the ground floor, though double glazing in a ground floor property reduces the risk of burglaries and offsets these fears to some extent.

4. A rental property on a busy main road need not be a turn-off for prospective tenants providing that it is double glazed to reduce traffic noise and it is not difficult to drive onto the road.

5. Rightly or wrongly, a high proportion of Social Security tenants in flats or multi-occupancy buildings carries a stigma which can limit the rent you charge.

6. Check, prior to purchase, that there are no clauses in the property contract that will prevent you letting. You may have to be persistent to obtain the documents from the solicitor, but it will prevent a lot of upset if you view the contract clauses at an early stage.

What should you look out for when you are starting letting ?

1. Even if you intend to manage the property yourself it is very advisable to use an agent to prepare the contract, select/vet the tenants and advise about bad tenants.

2. The agent must **ALWAYS** obtain a :
   - previous landlord's reference
   - bank reference
   - employer's reference
   - credit check
   - At least one month's deposit for any damage plus one month's rent in advance

3. In addition, use your common sense to do your own spot checks, e.g.:
   - If the tenant says that he is a Pharmacist, look in the local library reference section which will contain a list of Members of the Institute of Pharmacists,
   - If he is a member of a local club, try to find someone in the same club who will vouch for him.

4. Keep an agent between you and the tenant to prevent being identified as a personal target for any resentment they might harbor against landlords.

5. Aim for a high standard of furniture and furnishings. You will reap the reward in being able to charge higher rents and tenants are more likely to look after them.

6. Gas regulations have been strengthened over the last few years. They apply to leases of less than seven years and to licenses of residential property and not only cover appliances but also associated equipment (flues, installation pipe-work etc.)

Only a gas installer registered with CORGI should be used to carry out the required yearly checks. A copy of the record must be given to the tenant within 28 days of it being carried out.

This record should contain a list of required information which includes the companies approved registration number with the Health and Safety Executive.

Breach of the regulations is a criminal offence.

7. The landlord is legally responsible for ensuring that the electrical system and any appliances are safe. They should be checked by a qualified electrician prior to letting and at regular intervals thereafter.

8. All furniture must comply with the safety regulations which forbid dangerous materials being used in the upholstery. Furniture sold after 31 December 1996 will comply and should have tabs to verify the fact.

8. It is a legal requirement that the landlord must install smoke detectors in any rented property.

9. Don't decorate with strong colours. Tenants prefer a clean, neutral background on which they can impose their own identities.

10. Remember that your tenants are a crucial part of your business. Be formal with them but totally respect their privacy and sort out any problems they have immediately. This way you will get fewer and shorter gaps.

   To pre-empt problems it is worth identifying indirect ways to find out if they are happy, perhaps through a neighbor. This way you may be able to deter them from leaving at Xmas or early in the summer holidays when it is a bad time to get new tenants.

11. The insurance of the building, furniture and equipment, (if the latter are provided by the landlord), is his responsibility unless agreed otherwise.

12. Look for equal sized bedrooms which tenants can make better use of.

13. Normally a deposit of one months rent in advance **is** taken from the tenant to be held by whoever is managing the property, you or the agent.

   Some landlords take a little over one month's rent as deposit so that the tenant isn't tempted to use it as their final rental payment, leaving no money for repairs to damage. An extra £100 added to a £500 rental (or

£200 to a higher rent) can act as an effective deterrent.

14. In a furnished let the tenant will expect the property to contain all the necessary furniture, major appliances (not tv or stereo), kitchen equipment and sometimes bed linen.

Be aware of the rules regarding Multiple Occupation - HMO

If you propose to let a property to a group of people be aware that it could be classed by the local authority as a house in multiple occupation (HMO).

The legal definition of an HMO is one which is occupied by "persons who do not form a single household."

The regulations exclude families or groups of four people or less and they refer to any type of residential unit, not just a house.

Examples of HMOs are:
- student accommodation
- hostels and refuges
- flats with shared facilities
- besits or flatlets
- guest houses or B & Bs.

Local Authorities maintain an obligatory registration scheme for HMOs and require landlords to comply with a range of regulations ranging from fire escape requirements through to provision of details about occupants and proper management of the property.

In addition the landlord of an HMO must comply with obligatory statutes and regulations which address a wide range of safety and health issues including:

- cleanliness
- windows and ventilation facilities
- fire escapes and escape passages
- provision of rubbish bins and ensuring regular removal of rubbish
- safety of the property
- keeping shared facilities in proper working order
- maintaining the gas, electricity, water supply and drainage in proper working order.

Breach of these regulations could lead to prosecution.

Are there any particular contractual areas involving the tenants to be aware of ?

1. Take the advice of your agent about the most suitable type of contract and how to set it up.

2. An accurate and up to date register of the contents and condition of furniture and decor, signed by both landlord and tenant, is the first step to avoiding future disputes about the return of the deposit.

3. A turnover of tenant every year or 18 months need not be a bad thing, if rents generally are rising and you have strict vetting procedures and a good agent who minimises the gaps between tenants.

   If they are not rising a longer term contract will cut down on the number of gaps and reduce the rent lost while the property is empty.

4. Ensure that you understand the difference between "Wear and Tear", which you must accept, and "Accidental Damage" which a tenant must pay for out of the deposit.

   (This is described *in Pitfall 3—How to Minimise Wear and Tear*)

True Case Study

Mr. and Mrs. Holland were looking for a property to buy to rent out and were very impressed by a flat on the top floor of a six storey apartment block. It had a superb view over a landscaped park and an excellent layout, even though the kitchen was a little cramped.

The couple organised a structural survey which highlighted three major, worrying areas, namely:

- the structural concrete had been repaired but some reinforcement was still visible and rusting

- the lift was coming to the end of its useful life

- the flat roof had not been repaired for fifteen years, with a normal life expectancy of ten to fifteen years.

On checking the accounts, obtained from the Estate Agent that managed the block of flats, Mr. Holland found that there was only £5000 held as reserve in the management accounts to cover the cost of future repairs and maintenance.

In spite of the penthouse location and the beautiful view the couple did not put in an offer.

Issues That Really Matter

The previous Section described the key steps to buying and letting residential property.

Section 2 focuses on six key issues that must be understood if you are to become successful, namely :

- *Understanding Buy to Let finances*

- *Estimating the likely profits*

- *Minimising the risk*

- *Raising a loan*

- *Selecting an agent to manage the property*

- *Taxation of profits*

ISSUE 1
◆
Understand Buy to Let Finances

In order to invest in property successfully and avoid over stretching your finances you must understand:

- how property prices vary with time
- how rental returns vary
- the impact of interest rate changes.

How have property prices varied in the past?

Over the last 70 years property prices have risen on average by 7.7% annually. But the rate at which they have increased in individual years has varied considerably, going through a regular cycle of zero or low growth followed by a surge in prices usually lasting between six months and two years.

Following these surge, some property prices have dropped by around 10% but it is commonly felt that this is caused by people offloading properties they have bought at prices that were higher than their market value.

As an example - a two bedroom flat in an urban area of the North West went through the following price cycle in the late 1990's and early 2000.

		Value
	1995	£43,000
	1998	£48,000
	1999	£52,000
Spring	2001	£79,000
Autumn	2001	£75,000

What has been the return on rental property?

Over the cycle of 1995/2000 the average rental return from property before deduction of all expenses has gone from a peak of approximately 12% down to 7% and under .

(*Rental return is calculated by dividing the yearly rental income by the value of the property.*)

This large variation has mainly been caused by the fact that rents have only very gradually increased during the cycle in comparison with the high increases in the value of the properties being rented.

How have interest rates varied in the past?

Interest rate levels in the UK are predominantly influenced by the international economy which causes rates to rise and fall through what appears to be a random a series of cycles.

These cycles are difficult to predict and have in the past caused the bank base rates to rise as high as 12% with occasional surges even higher.

Use these facts to manage your Buy to Let finances

1. Invest long term

At certain points in the afore mentioned property price cycles, even if you have followed all the guide lines in this book, you may find that the margin between the rental return and what you pay in interest shrinks dramatically.

You must take the long term view that provided you can cautiously cover your outgoings and prices continue to follow historical trends you are likely to get approximately 7% average capital growth per year.

At a later point in the cycle rental levels should catch up and provide additional income.

2. Invest at the right time

To take best advantage of the property price cycles you must purchase your properties before the surges take place.

Looking at the previous example of a property in the North West:

		Value	Increase
	1995	£43,000	
	1998	£48,000	11.6%
	1999	£52,000	9.3%
Spring	2001	£79,000	63.8%
Autumn	2001	£75,000	-9.3%

Between 1995 and 1999 the property only increased in price in total by 21%, but the property surged by 63% from 1999 to 2001.

3. Guard against interest rate rises.

The biggest financial risk, that is out of your control, is that interest rates may surge to 12% or more while your rental is tied or at the worst you have no tenant at all.

A fixed rate mortgage will help you to avoid this situation but it will not enable you to benefit from falling interest rates.

A strategy that some landlords take is :

- when interest rates are low a proportion of the loan is taken out on variable rates while the remainder is on a fixed rate, checking that they can cope financially if the variable interest rate rises to a far higher figure

- when interest rates are high the properties are purchased with a lower fixed rate proportion of the loan. By ensuring that the variable rate mortgage has no redemption penalties you can switch to a higher proportion of fixed rate when interest rates drop.

4. Guard against over-stretching your finances

The second biggest risk is that you will get carried away by over confidence and take on too many properties as lenders begin to trust you more and offer you loans at commercial rates.

The future is very difficult to predict and rental income could decline in future for a variety of reasons including:

- an over supply of Buy to Let properties and

- possible changes in Government tax policies such as elimination of mortgage interest as deductible against rental profit

By focusing on the following key points you will cut down the risk of over-stretching your finances:

- Purchase quality properties close to good transport links so that at worst you will stand a better chance of selling

- Ensure that the rental income exceeds all the outgoings by sufficient to allow for at least a one month gap in rental payments each year

- Feedback from Agents is that the majority of Landlords restrict their portfolios to four flats. Above this figure the risks multiply considerably.

Key Steps to building a larger portfolio.

There are a number of tried and tested steps to building a larger property portfolio, including:

- Get to know your local Estate Agents to identify the properties that are easily rentable and which will increase quickest in value

- Monitor the property price cycles diligently, buying at the end of the period when prices are level or slowly rising - before they begin to surge **

*(** The Land Registry website has historical data on typical property values which can be used to calculate price rises - on www.landreg.gov.uk or 0845 308 4545.)*

- At the end of each price rise cycle use the spare capital as collateral to buy more properties

- Identify new developments even before Planning Approval has been granted. Developers are often desperate for cash flow at this stage and may give up to 15% discount.

- Take out interest only loans, using all your resources to maximise the capital you borrow

- Follow the rules in this book that guide you towards

cutting down gaps between tenants. Every extra month's rent each year can be used as a deposit to borrow further capital

- The more properties you acquire the more you must check and recheck the safety factors in your financial calculations - looking at worst scenarios

- DON'T get carried away by over-confidence when you find that loans become increasingly easy to arrange.

True Case Study

Mr. Barker paid off his house, valued at £135K, by the age of 48 by making extra capital payments each year and using a redundancy payout.

Because of the small amount he had paid into a pension scheme he set about purchasing four properties to rent as follows:

He first purchased two flats at £43K and £43.5K, borrowing £95K for the cost of the properties plus renovation plus furniture, using his existing home as security.

Concerned about mortgages rising he arranged to split his mortgage, fully repayable over 12 years as follows:

Sum of £10K - variable interest rate loan
Sum of £83K - loan with interest rate fixed for 5 years

Five years later the flats were valued at £75K each, with no debt tied to them so he could use 90% of their value to borrow against.

He decided to purchase two more flats at a higher price of £95K each to spread his portfolio and look more towards capital appreciation.

Within 3 months they increased to £110K each. His borrowings were as follows:

Secured on	Total Value	Loan	Type
Residence	£175K	£93K	£10K variable £83K% fixed (repay over 12 years)
Flats 1 & 2	£150K	£135K	Interest only - fixed rate
Flat 3	£110K	£65K	Interest only - variable rate
Flat 4	£110K	0	
TOTAL	**£545**	**£293**	£75K fixed £218K variable

Based on current values his return on capital is 7.5%, excluding any capital appreciation which is currently at a low of 2.5%.

ISSUE 2

◆

Estimating the Likely Profits

In advance of buying your first property, the likely, average profits can be estimated by focusing on the four key areas of :

- rental income
- property outgoings
- loan charges
- management charges

How would you estimate the likely rental income?

The starting point is to contact estate agents, look in local newspapers and go round properties to let. This way you will quickly develop a feel for rental levels for different standards of accommodation in the areas you are considering.

The following guide-lines will help you to calculate the likely income, provided you :

- buy the property in an area which is attractive to the type of client you wish to let to

- keep the quality of furnishings at a sufficiently high level to satisfy these clients

- treat your tenants well
- carefully select and monitor your agent.

Income from flats, bed-sits and houses?

Net income for these three types of property varies considerably, as shown previously.

For estimating purposes agents normally assume that they will be able to let desirable properties for 11 months of each year. This should be achievable provided you follow the previously mentioned guidelines.

Income from corporate clients?

Corporate clients require a far higher standard of property, furnished to match.

To deliver this standard you will need a premium of 25 to 35% over and above average rental values, half of which could well be spent on keeping it up to scratch.

Unless you can manage to purchase a property in an area where a high occupancy rate is virtually guaranteed it is best to assume that the net income will be much the same as a professional let. Any extra profit will then be a bonus.

Income from student accommodation?

Renting to students can be far more profitable than to non students simply because you don't have to pay extra to suit demanding tenants and you can fit more tenants in one building. Also you only need one kitchen and bathroom per five students, unlike self-contained bed-sits which require more space within each unit.

To calculate the likely profits, students are charged full rent during the term. During holidays they either pay full rent, half rent or a retainer, depending upon local demand.

The local ground rules can easily be identified by requesting information from a number of agents in the area that you wish to buy your property, pretending to be a student or a student's parent.

The normal college year is usually 32 weeks, or 34 in certain areas. Again this can be pinned down by phoning the particular college in the area that you are considering.

Example of student rental income calculations.

Students are charged full rent during the term. During holidays they either pay full rent, half rent or a retainer, depending upon local demand. In this example we have assumed a payment of half the rent to be paid during the holidays. The normal college year is usually 32 weeks or 34 in certain areas. In this example we have assumed 32 weeks.

A house is rented to 4 students at £50 each per week per person.

Full rental income per year
        = 32 weeks * 4 students * £50 = £6400

Retainer during holidays
        = 20 weeks * 4 students * £25 = £2000

        Total yearly income   = £8400

What property outgoings should you allow for in estimating likely profit ?

The following outgoings related to the property must be deducted from the rental in calculating the profit :

**Deduct maintenance costs, service charges and
 wear and tear.**

Maintenance costs cover not only maintenance of the fabric of the building, but also things such as gardening, painting external window frames and doors, unblocking drains and work in common areas.

In the case of apartments, these costs are usually included in the service charge paid to the organisation that manages the upkeep of the properties, along with electricity to common areas, insurance of the property and agent's fees for managing the estate. In addition the service charge usually includes an extra charge which is set aside to cover any future bills such as periodic roof repairs or replacement of a lift.

Service charges for apartments are paid by the landlord. Typical figures are readily available from estate agents and provided you have chosen a property in good condition and you have checked that the management accounts contain sufficient capital reserve to cover the long term bills the risk of future surprise bills is reduced.

If you intend to look after the maintenance of a property yourself, you would be well advised to build up your own reserve fund for future maintenance work, setting aside money from the rent each month.

To cover the future cost of wear and tear of furnishings, furniture and decorations a similar fund needs to be set aside.

Deduct rates and heating costs.

Most rental agreements specify that the tenant pays for domestic and water rates. So they will only come into the calculation of profit if there is a gap between tenants, when you will be obliged to pay domestic and water rates plus any heating costs necessary to prevent the water pipes freezing.

For estimating purposes, assume gaps will amount to two months per year, less will be a bonus.

Other outgoings to deduct to calculate profit

Other outgoings which will need to be deducted are contents insurance and property insurance unless the latter is included in a service charge.

What loan payments should you allow for in estimating likely profit?

Unless you have opted for an interest only mortgage the loan payments will be made up of two parts :

- capital repayments and
- interest repayments.

But only the interest repayments should be taken into account in the profit calculation. (This is not to say that you should not take both payments into account when calculating whether you can afford the loan.)

What agent's management charges should you allow for in estimating likely profit ?

The level of the agent's management fees will depend entirely upon how much work you intend an agent to do and how much you will do yourself. (See *Issue 5—Selecting an Agent.*)

Assuming that you will use an agent to obtain and vet the tenants while you manage the property during the letting period, an agent's management charge of 10%, including VAT, of the yearly rental will be a reasonable target to aim for.

Example of agents fees.

eg. Rental for 11 months of the year
$$= 11 \text{ months} * £550 \qquad = £6050$$

Agents yearly fees will be 10% of this figure $\quad = £605$

Example of profit calculations

For an apartment valued at £70,000, with a monthly rental of £570 and £47 service charge, assuming 11 months average letting per year

Yearly rental income
= 11 months @ £570 per month   = £6270

Gross outgoings
Yearly service charges = 12 months @ £47 = -£564

Set aside wear & tear fund 5% of rent   = -£314
           Gross Profit   £5392

Gross Profit as a % of apartment's value
$$= \frac{5392 *100}{80,000} \qquad = 6.74\%$$

Net outgoings

Agents letting fees   = £600
Loan interest repayment   = £3850
        TOTAL   £4450

Net Profit   £5392 - £4450   = £942

The owner in this example is now using the profit after deduction of tax to put towards the monthly loan payments to purchase the property as part of his pension plans.

ISSUE 3

◆

Minimising the Risks

In the United Kingdom, property is considered a safe, long term investment. In spite of this, no investment is totally without risk. But by knowing which risks are most likely to arise, you can move forward cautiously, taking positive steps to minimise them.

The main risks, in the residential property rental business, fall into the two categories of Rental Income Risks and Outgoings Risks.

How can you reduce the risk of your rental income falling ?

1. Reduce the risk of the tenants defaulting on their rental payment.

- use an agent to vet the tenants, prepare the contract and act as an interface between you and them

- take at least one month's deposit plus one month's rental in advance.

- treat your tenants well and they will be more likely to look after your property.

2. Reduce the length of the gaps between tenants when no rental income is coming in.

- select the property in as desirable area as you can afford and provide a standard of furnishings that tenants will be happy with

- advertise the property, or check that your agent is doing so, in advance of the tenant leaving, even if this means more inconvenience arranging evening viewings to fit in with the tenant

- fix your rental level so that it is slightly lower than the market level for similar properties to rent in the area.

3. Avoid a general decline in rental levels.

- high quality rental accommodation in desirable areas will be less likely to suffer declining rental levels

- go for a mortgage without redemption penalties that allows you to use surplus rental income to make over-payments on the mortgage. This accelerated payment of the debt will create a surplus which can be used if rental income falls in the future.

How can you reduce the risk of your financial outgoings increasing ?

1. Due to an interest rates increase.

- Consider taking out a fixed rate loan for a long enough period to enable your own income to rise or for rents to increase

- accelerated repayments of mortgage debt will mean that funds can be set aside to cover future increases in interest rates.

2. Due to damage to the property and wear and tear.

- be sure to fully understand the difference between damage and wear and tear, by studying *Pitfall 3 - How to minimise Wear and Tear*

- set aside a reserve fund to cover future wear and tear

- Take at least one month's deposit to cover any damage.

ISSUE 4

♦

Raising a Loan

Over the last few years, banks and building societies have become more flexible and orientated to their customers' needs, especially for the purchase of rental properties.

Many will even give interest only loans to landlords with only three or four years experience.

How do you go about raising a loan to purchase your first property to rent ?

A loan to purchase a property to rent can be taken out in two different ways, using either the security of your own home or through a buy to let scheme which normally uses the security of the new property.

In both cases you will have to prove to the bank or building society that you have sufficient income to make the repayments and that your loan does not exceed a certain percentage of the property value.

But the main difference between the two options is that mortgages based on the security of a rental property usually require a 10 to 20% deposit and the rental income to be sufficient to cover the mortgage payments plus 25 to

30% in case no rent is coming in.

What rules will apply if you raise the loan using your own home as security ?

The rules will vary from lender to lender but they are usually exactly the same as if you were going for a new mortgage or a mortgage extension. That is to say :

- the loan should not exceed a figure specified by the lender, usually about 3 to 3.5 times the main income or 2.5 times the main income plus other incomes

- the loan should not exceed a specific percentage of the value of the property, (usually 90% or 95%.)

- the rental income may or may not be taken into account, dependent upon the lender's own rules.

What rules will apply if you raise the loan using the rental property as security ?

Again the rules vary from lender to lender but the norm is that :
- most lenders require a deposit of 10 to 20% of the mortgage sum

- lenders prefer the rent to be 25 to 30% more than the mortgage payments to allow for other costs such as wear and tear, whilst building in some flexibility in case interest rates rise or there are gaps when no rent is coming in.

What types of loans are available ?

For a mortgage using your house or the rented property as security, borrowers can chose from a range of interest rate options including :

Capped Rate Loans, where the payments will rise or fall as interest rates vary, but there will be a capped upper and/or lower limit.

Variable Rate Loans where the payments will rise or fall with interest rate fluctuations, with no maximum limit.

Fixed Rate Loans where the interest rate and hence the payments remain constant for a specified number of years, after which they normally revert to a variable rate loan unless an alternative is agreed.

What repayment method will you chose ?

In addition to deciding on the type of loan to go for you need to decide on the repayment method.
You can choose to go for capital and interest repayments where the interest and a proportion of the debt are paid off each month; or interest only payments where interest is paid each month but the capital may or may not have to be repaid in one go at the end of the mortgage term.

In the latter case, to repay the capital, you will need to contribute to an endowment or personal equity investment plan. Alternatively you could sell or re-mortgage the property in the same way that many property companies operate.

It is worth remembering that interest can be offset against rental income for tax purposes. So there is less incentive to go for a capital and interest repayment mortgage where the interest reduces each month.

This booklet cannot provide financial advice about these alternatives - an independent, qualified Financial Adviser is the best person to do that. But certain facts are worth bearing in mind :
1. A fixed rate loan might be more costly in the long run, but it could stop you becoming insolvent if interest rates should rise dramatically.

2. Beware of redemption penalties which will prevent you

repaying extra capital. You may not wish to do so at the moment but what if you do so in 5 years time.

3. Check what the interest rate will be at the end of any fixed rate period. But be sure that the rate is tied into the base rate, not solely left to the lenders discretion.

4. A quick way to check mortgage deals available is through the Financial Section of the Sunday Papers.

True Case Study

Mr. Egerton wanted to buy a property to rent but he had no cash savings whatsoever to put down as a deposit. He had only got £35,000 outstanding to repay on his house, valued at £98,000.

His salary was £20,000, while his wife's salary was £12,000.

Having no deposit, Mr. Egerton could only go for a mortgage using his own house as security.

The maximum mortgage he could go for was :

3 times his salary	=	£72,000
plus his wives salary	=	£12,000
plus the expected property income	=	£5,000 **
TOTAL		£89,000

*(** Not all lenders will allow this to be included.)*

The lender also specified that he could only borrow up to 95% of the value of his house eg. £93,000.

The maximum amount that Mr Egerton could borrow was the lower of:

$$£89,000 - £35,000 = £54,000$$
$$\text{or} \quad £93,000 - £35,000 = £58,000 \quad \text{eg. } £54,000$$

After considering all his outgoings, and his income, Mr. Egerton decided to go for a single bedroom flat, costing £50,000, which, he checked, would bring in a rental of £400 per month, taking the precaution of taking out insurance to cover his death, long term sickness or redundancy.

ISSUE 5
◆
Selecting an Agent

Should you use an agent to manage the letting ?

In spite of the introduction of the Assured Shorthold Tenancy contract, which has given owners the right to regain possession, the law relating to landlord and tenant is still complicated.

So it is highly advisable to use an agent's wealth of experience during the first few years that you are learning - BUT not just any agent.

However competent the agent you choose, his prime motive will be to earn a living - which means that he needs as many clients as possible and he needs to keep his staff costs down.

Bearing this in mind, you need to take great care in selecting your agent and in monitoring that they deliver what they are being paid to deliver.

Is there a guaranteed way of selecting a good agent ?

By selection through the Association of Residential Letting Agents, (ARLA), the National Association of Estate Agents (NAEA) or the Royal Institute of Chartered Surveyors (RICS) you will obtain an agent who belongs to a reputable organisation that works to strict rules of conduct.

The former organisation, ARLA, specialises in residential letting but members of the other organisations are equally experienced in this field.

Regardless of how you select the agent you must ensure that you get his or her full commitment.

A lack of commitment could lead to bigger gaps between tenancies which will in turn lead to reduced rental income. The normal gap between tenancies, is often quoted as one month, but a committed agent can reduce this to zero -

which could mean large savings over a 10 year period.

How should you select an agent and ensure that you receive good service ?

1. Don't automatically select the managing agent who charges the least.

   Your aim should be to maximise your rental return, so you must select an agent who will attract prospective tenants who are prepared to and capable of paying the level of rents that you are seeking.

   Look at the agent's shop frontage, its decor, the properties being advertised and try to imagine what a potential tenant's impression of the agent would be. Prospective tenants are cautious about approaching an agent. They fear the worst and will easily be put off by a shabby shop-where the staff lack customer-care skills

2. Find out what rental market the agent specialises in. Agents often concentrate on particular areas, such as social security tenants, company employee transfers or tenants in specific income levels. They might insist that they cover all areas but their image alone will tell you where their main focus is.

   This is very important because the agent will tend to recruit and treat your tenants in a similar manner to their other tenants, which could have a big effect upon your tenant turnover and hence the numbers of gaps between tenancies.

3. Use your instincts in selecting the agent. Go into their office, and spend some time explaining your requirements.

   If you notice the following - do not be overfaced just politely explain that you are speaking to a number of agents and then leave.

   - Their desk is untidy with disorderly paperwork

   - They are patronising and do not seem prepared to discuss things openly

   - They do not make you feel relaxed

   - Their staff appear discourteous

   Remember that all these characteristics will also be shown to your tenants, leading to a higher risk of confrontation and higher tenant turnover.

   You are more likely to make a profit if you employ an agent, at reasonable fees, who will pick the right tenants, maximise the rent and minimise the gaps between lettings.

4. Negotiate his fees in line with his work scope.

Agents' fees are negotiable but they normally fall within the following ranges as a percentage of the rental.

8% to 12% (including VAT) **- Selecting tenants including :**
- Interview and select a tenant
- Prepare the contract
- Agree the terms and conditions of the contract between you and the tenant
- Advertise early enough to minimise gaps between tenants
- Interview prospective tenants and weed out problem cases
- Obtain bank, employer's and previous landlord's references, credit check and Magistrate's Court case search.
- Arrange contract signing and registration with Land Registry, obtain deposit, one month's advance rent and set up standing orders for rental payment.

8% to 15% (including VAT) **- Select and manage the** tenants (including the tasks previously described) **plus:**
- Act as a barrier between you and the tenant
- Do regular checks on the condition of the property.
- Check that the rent is paid on time and passed to you
- Organise repairs

10% to 20% (including VAT) - **Select and manage the tenants (including the tasks previously described) plus managing the accounts plus :**
- Prepare an end of year accounts balance
- Prepare an Inland Revenue statement of accounts.

When to pay the agent ?

It is preferable to have an arrangement where you pay the agent monthly upon receipt of the tenant's rent, rather than all up front when the tenant signs the contract.

Most agents will agree to this - no rent no fee - but they will not volunteer the arrangement.

Example :
An Agent's quoted fee of 12%, means that he will charge 12% of the rental payable during the period of the contract.

e.g. If the term of the rental contract is 6 months and the monthly rental is £500.

Rental for the contract period is 6 times £500 = £3000
The agents monthly fee will be :

$$\text{12\% of £500} \qquad = \quad £60$$

The £60 will only include VAT if it has been previously agreed. Otherwise it will be charged extra.

Thoughts before final selection of the agent

In making the final selection of the agent and deciding on the extent of his duties, take into account:

1. You only need one tenant to refuse to vacate the property to realise that the loss of rental could make the agent's fees seem very small.

2. A good agent will save you money by ensuring that gaps between lets are kept to a minimum.

3. Before deciding to do the work of an agent, make a realistic estimate of the time you have available.

4. If you do decide to use an agent solely for selecting and vetting the tenants it is preferable to be able to call on his advice during the management period.

Some accredited organisations whose members manage properties are:

Association of Residential Letting Agents, Maple House, Woodside Road, Amersham, Bucks, HP6 6AA

Royal Institute of Chartered Surveyors
12 Great George Street, London, SW1P 3AD

Small Landlords Assoc.,73 Upper Richmond Street, London, SW15 2SZ)
National Association of Estate Agents
Arbon House, 21 Jury Street, Warwick, CV34 4EH

__True Case Study__

Selecting an Agent

Mr. Round started renting in a small way, with a terraced house left to him on his mother's death. In the first 18 months he used three agents, one after another.

The first charged 15% plus VAT solely for obtaining and vetting the tenant, organising the contract; the inventory; the deposit and the standing orders, leaving Mr. Round to manage it during the letting period. Mr. Round tried unsuccessfully to negotiate a lower fee when the first tenant left, so he switched to another agent.

The second agent charged 10% (excluding VAT) for the same services, but he seemed disorganised from the outset and failed to advertise the property early enough at the end of the rental term. So the gap between tenants, when Mr. Round was receiving no rent, extended to six weeks. The agent also seemed to have a marked preference for Social Security tenants, even though the property could have commanded a higher rent from professional couples.

Mr. Round finally settled on an agent who focused on renting to young professional couples and covered the same work scope for 10% including VAT, in addition to :

- acting as an interface between Mr. Round and the

tenants during the period that Mr. Round managed the house

- providing advice about any problems that might arise with the tenants

With the negligible amount of time needed to manage young professional couples as tenants the arrangement has worked well. The only hiccup was a dispute about wear and tear which was quickly resolved with the advice of the agent.

ISSUE 6

◆

Taxation of Profits

How to keep the tax you pay to a minimum

The secret to minimising the tax you will have to pay is to :
- know exactly what you can put forward for tax relief and
- keep good records of income and expenditure, right from the first moment that you think about becoming a landlord.

To reap the full dividend you need to keep every invoice and scrap of relevant information filed away carefully.
What taxes will you be liable to pay?

Tax levied on your rental property falls into two categories - **Tax on Rental Income** and **Capital Gains Tax** payable if you sell the property.

What tax will you pay on your rental income ?

This will be calculated, based on the rental income received within each tax year, after deduction of allowable expenses, provided that the property is available for letting for at least 140 days per year or 70 days a year on short term lets not exceeding 30 days each.

Full details of the up to date regulations and allowable expenses are given in the Inland Revenue Practitioner's Series, IR150, available from your local Inland Revenue Office.

Briefly, they must be "incurred wholly and exclusively for business purposes and not be of a capital nature."

Allowable deductions against rental income include :

- Agent's letting and management fees not included elsewhere

- Interest paid on the loan to purchase the property above the Inland Revenue limit on your own residence.
- Wear and tear relating to furniture and furnishings, TVs, fridges and freezers, carpets and floor coverings, curtains, linen, crockery or cutlery, cookers, washing machines and dishwashers etc.

  (The above figure can be calculated from actual figures or estimated as 10% of the yearly rental after deduction of certain charges and services that would normally be paid by the tenant, (e.g. domestic tax, water rates.))

- Ordinary expenditure on repairs such as :
  * roof repairs due to storm damage
  * maintenance of the buildings or grounds
  * periodic maintenance such as stone cleaning and re-pointing
  * damp and rot treatment
  * mending broken windows, doors, furniture and machines such as lifts and cookers
  * replacing wooden beams with steel girders, lead pipes with copper or plastic, single glazed soft-wood windows with single glazed PVC windows.
- Building and contents insurance
- Domestic, water and sewerage rates paid by the owner
- Service charges paid by the landlord
- Solicitor's charges incurred in organising the loan
- Costs of periodic redecorating
- Items such as petrol and train fares incurred for business purposes associated with your property.

What tax will you pay on capital gains made on the property ?

Legislation relating to capital gains is complex and for all but the most straight forward cases specialist advice should be sought. In general, tax will be levied on any increase in value of the property when you eventually dispose of it after deducting :

- an allowance for inflation increases that would have taken place over the same period

- the cost of improvements carried out during that period, but not including wear and tear, which is covered under tax on rental income. Examples of improvements are :
  * central heating installation
  * replacement of single glazing by double glazing
  * a new kitchen

- Solicitor's and estate agent's fees in buying and selling the property

- costs incurred in Surveyor's and/or Structural Engineer's surveys

- items such as petrol, train fares which were necessary to select and purchase the property

Example of a Tax Statement

RENTAL INCOME STATEMENT
Flat 8, Seathwaite Court, Hale Road, Manchester

Income
Rent from property	£6600

AllowableExpenses
Rent, rates, contents insurance	-£757
(service charge £564)	
(contents insurance £140)	
(domestic & water rates during gaps £53**)	
Repairs, maintenance, renewals	
(lock repair £75)	-£75
Finance charges	-£2300
(interest on loans to purchase the property)	
Legal & professional costs	-£660
(agents fees - £660)	
Other expenses	-£12
IR allowance for Wear and tear	
(10% of £6600 less £53** see above)	<u>-£607</u>
Taxable income	£2189

There are ways that this figure of £2189 might be reduced, but legitimate tax avoidance is a highly complex subject.

An accountant will advise you, but be aware of the costs of setting up any partnership or company, including accountant's fees and possibly national insurance payments as a self employed person.

Remember also that you will be taxed at your highest tax rate on both your rental income and on any capital gains. (For specific details - refer to :

Taxation of Rents - A guide to property income
Inland Revenue Practitioner Series IR 150
Obtainable from your local Inland Revenue Office.)

Avoiding the Most Common Pitfalls

There is nothing like learning from experience, provided it is not painful experience.

Section 3 provides advice in the areas that cause most problems, namely :

- *Avoiding disputes relating to the deposit*

- *Cutting down gaps between tenants*

- *Minimising wear and tear*

- *Watching the trends*

- *Avoiding the gross yield trap*

- *Planning long term.*

PITFALL 1
◆
Avoiding Disputes About the Deposit

Disputes about the return of the Deposit, - often linked to disputes over Wear and Tear - are one of the most common causes of arguments between owners and tenants.

How can you prevent disputes about the deposit ?

1. Always obtain a deposit equivalent at least to one month's rent in advance against accidental or malicious damage.

2. Be sure to understand the difference between normal wear and tear, which is not recoverable from the deposit and accidental or malicious damage, which is. (*See Pitfall 3*)

3. Ensure that the rental agreement clearly states the purpose of the deposit.

4. Deterioration of decorations due to tenants smoking. may be classed as wear and tear if you don't put a clause in the contract that prohibits smoking.

Similarly you should expect more wear and tear if you accept tenants with children.

One way of covering the cost of this extra wear and tear is by including in the contract clauses that require the tenant to pay for the cost of redecoration before the end of the contract.

5. Give the tenant the opportunity to repair any accidental or malicious damage during the term of the agreement. If they choose not to do so during that period you can repair the damage yourself and deduct the full cost out of the deposit.

6. In a dispute do not be drawn into lengthy written explanations which could be turned against you. Discuss the issue with your agent, decide whether the damage is really wear and tear or damage and, as a last resort, go to arbitration through the Association of Residential Letting Agents before getting drawn into legal proceedings.

PITFALL 2

♦

Minimising Gaps Between Tenants

For every week that your property has no tenant you will be losing rent, in addition to paying domestic and water rates and possibly heating to stop the pipes freezing.

Unless rental levels are rising rapidly you must minimise the turnover of tenants and keep the gaps between tenants as short as possible.

To cut down tenant turnover :
- buy the property in a desirable area
- don't charge more than the going rate for the locality
- maintain a reasonable standard of furnishing and decor
- keep the agent between you and the tenant
- treat the tenant as you would expect to be treated.

To keep the gaps between tenants to a minimum:
- chose your agent carefully
- check that he advertises for new tenants prior to the existing tenant leaving
- do not let your agent consider anyone who is not prepared to put down a deposit to secure the property.

PITFALL 3

◆

How to Minimise Wear and Tear

The most common disputes that arises between landlord and tenant are disagreements over the meaning of **Wear and Tear** and **Accidental Damage**.

As a general rule accidental or malicious damage that is not repaired by the tenant during the term of the rental agreement, can be repaired by the landlord and the cost taken out of the deposit - while wear and tear cannot.

Examples of accidental or malicious damage recoverable from the deposit are :

- putting a hot pan onto a kitchen surface which burns through the laminate
- smashing a porcelain vase or lamp stand
- breaking a chair leg
- cigarette burns to the sofa.

Examples of normal wear and tear that cannot be recovered from the deposit are :

Normal deterioration of items such as :

- carpets
- mechanical items such as cookers, fridges, freezers

- cutlery and crockery
- floor coverings and curtains
- decorations

Grey areas regarding the deposit.

There are a number of grey areas where disputes arise and a court is likely to rule that the deposit cannot be used to pay for work, including :

- darkening of a room due to smokers when you were fully aware that the prospective tenants smoked and smoking is not forbidden under the terms and conditions of the rental agreement

- damage to skirting boards and decorations caused by children when you were fully aware that they would be in the flat.

How to avoid arguments about wear and tear ?

The key to the issue of wear and tear or damage is the Inventory.

To avoid disputes you must prepare a newly typed inventory for each new tenant detailing all the contents of the flat as well as the condition of the furniture, fixtures and fittings. The inventory should be passed to the tenant for checking, with a time limit of 7 days to make and agree any amendments to it.

What other ways can you cut down wear and tear ?

The following guidelines will help to reduce wear and tear:

1. Professional people and employees of reputable companies tend to cause less wear and tear as tenants.

2. Don't take tenants who are smokers or who have children or pets unless you accept that wear and tear will be higher.

3. Couples tend to be more house proud and cause less damage than single people.

4. Use your own initiative to check the background of a prospective tenant.

5. Keeping the agent as a barrier between you and the tenant will lead to less emotional involvement and reduce the risk of the tenant taking any resentment out on the property.

PITFALL 4

◆

Watch the Trends

Develop an understanding of the major characteristics that
will influence the type of property that you purchase and
the location you select.

Cultivate every possible opportunity to talk to your letting
agent or the valuer who comes to look at the properties
you are planning to purchase. They posses, literally, a
wealth of information.

They have inside knowledge about the geographical areas
that are rising and falling in popularity and can advise
which areas to concentrate on.

They also know the local preferences:

- Areas of over and under supply of particular types of
  property

- Whether local Universities and Colleges are going
  into the property market to help their students

- Any moves that the college is taking to relocate
  its departments outside the city

PITFALL 5

◆

Avoid the Gross Yield Trap

When you estimate the likely return, don't fall into the trap of looking at Gross Yield which is commonly quoted in the newspapers but does not take into account costs such as management fees, maintenance costs and gaps between tenants.

Net yields, taking costs such as these into account, will shave several percentages off your gross figure.

PITFALL 6

◆

Don't Think Short Term

The property market goes through cycles of boom and stagnation when prices and rents vary in line with the state of the national economy and people's perceptions of what is going to happen in the future.

Provided you offer premises to rent that are at the higher end of a particular market you will stand a far better chance of attracting and keeping good tenants. This will shelter you from the cyclic trends.

Treat your property as a long term investment, confident in the knowledge that there has been an overall rise in values and rental levels over the last fifty years .

Equally important, renting is becoming more socially acceptable in the UK. It has now risen to over 12% of the UK property market which is only a fraction of the 40% of people who rent in Germany.

ANNEX 1

Further Reading

Books about buying and renting residential property tend either to be background reading or to act as a reference source about specific areas.

Recommended Background Reading

Two practical books that cover buying, selling, renovating and letting property, available from most bookshops, are:

How to make money from your property by Adam Walker from "How To Books."

How to make money from your property by Fiona Fullerton from Piatkus Books.

Recommended Reference Sources

Taxation of Rents - A guide to property income
Inland Revenue Practitioner Series IR 150
Obtainable from your local Inland Revenue Office

The Which Guide to Renting and Letting by Peter Wilde and Paul Butt available from most bookshops